# SUPER SPORTS STAR
# JEROME BETTIS

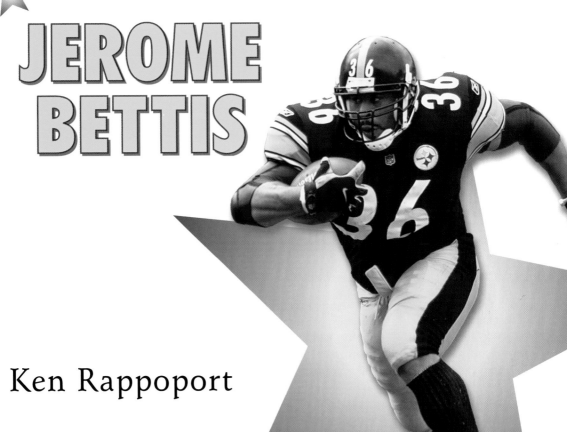

Ken Rappoport

**Enslow Publishers, Inc.**

40 Industrial Road        PO Box 38
Box 398              Aldershot
Berkeley Heights, NJ 07922   Hants GU12 6BP
USA                        UK

       http://www.enslow.com

**Library of Congress Cataloging-in-Publication Data**

Rappoport, Ken.
  Super sports star Jerome Bettis / Ken Rappoport.
     p. cm. — (Super sports star)
  Summary: Discusses the career of Jerome Bettis, the running back who was traded
from the St. Louis Rams to the Pittsburgh Steelers.
  Includes bibliographical references and index.
   ISBN 0-7660-2053-3
  1.  Bettis, Jerome—Juvenile literature.  2.  Football players—United
States—Juvenile literature. [1. Bettis, Jerome. 2. Football players.]
I. Title: Jerome Bettis. II. Title. III. Series.
   GV939.B48 R36 2003
   796.332'092—dc21                              2002008922

Printed in the United States of America

10 9 8 7 6 5 4 3 2 1

**To Our Readers:**
We have done our best to make sure all Internet Addresses in this book were active and
appropriate when we went to press. However, the author and the publisher have no
control over and assume no liability for the material available on those Internet sites or
on other Web sites they may link to. Any comments or suggestions can be sent by e-mail
to comments@enslow.com or to the address on the back cover.

**Photo Credits:** © Bill Amatucci/NFL Photos, p. 41; © Scott Boehm/NFL Photos,
p. 30; © Peter Brouillet/NFL Photos, pp. 14, 26, 39; © Christopher Condon/NFL
Photos, p. 38; © Chris Covatta/NFL Photos, p. 18; © Greg Crisp/NFL Photos,
pp. 6, 43; © Scott Cunningham/NFL Photos, p. 16; © Gerald Gallegos/NFL
Photos, p. 8; © George Gojkovich/NFL Photos, p. 28; © John Grieshop/NFL
Photos, p. 10; © Paul Jasienski/NFL Photos, pp. 12, 24; © Allen Kee/NFL Photos,
pp. 4, 32, 37; © Mark Konezny/NFL Photos, p. 34; © Marty Morrow/NFL
Photos, p. 7; © Bernie Nunez/NFL Photos, p. 22; © David Stluka/NFL Photos,
p. 20; © Ron Vesely/NFL Photos, p. 1.

**Cover Photo:** © Ron Vesely/NFL Photos.

# CONTENTS

# Introduction

His nickname is "The Bus." Meet Jerome Bettis. He is a running back for the Pittsburgh Steelers in the National Football League (NFL).

Like a bus, the 5-foot-11, 255-pound Bettis is not easy to stop. The reason is that he combines speed and power.

Bettis looks like two kinds of running backs rolled into one player. He can play fullback and get a couple of tough yards inside. He can be a tailback and break open a game with a long run. He is also a good pass catcher and a powerful blocking back for other runners.

Bettis can usually be counted on to rush for over 1,000-yards every season. That is the standard for top running backs in the NFL. In his first nine seaons in the NFL, Bettis only missed the 1,000-yard mark once. That was because he was hurt. He has worked hard to become one of the National Football League's top running backs.

# CHAPTER 1

# Ramming the Rams

The crowd roared as the Pittsburgh Steelers broke out of their huddle. It was second-and-three at the 50-yard line. The quarterback called a running play. Jerome Bettis was ready.

"I wanted to show I was a game-breaker," Bettis said.

It was November 4, 1996. The Steelers were facing the St. Louis Rams. It was just another game for the Steelers. But not just another game for Bettis.

Bettis used to play for the Rams. This

was his first game against them since they traded him to Pittsburgh. Bettis was hurt by the trade. The Rams said Bettis had slowed down and that he was not the "game-breaker" they needed. The Rams wanted someone who could turn a game around with one long run.

Bettis had been the Rams' No. 1 pick in the 1993 National Football League (NFL) draft. The NFL draft is the way professional football teams pick new players each year. At that time, the Rams were playing in Los Angeles. Bettis

Jerome Bettis surges downfield on his way to scoring another touchdown.

lived up to their hopes in his first season. He was named the NFL's Rookie of the Year. Bettis shared the title with Seattle quarterback Rick Mirer. But two years later, Bettis had a contract battle with the team. After a poor season in 1995, he was traded to Pittsburgh.

Bettis circled the 1996 Rams game on his calendar and now that day was here. Bettis wanted to show the Rams they had made a mistake in letting him go. So far, so good. He had already scored a

Even after Jerome Bettis won the NFL's Rookie of the Year award with the Rams, they still traded him to the Pittsburgh Steelers.

touchdown on a short run. Now the Steelers were on the 50-yard line.

The Steelers lined up in a power formation to the left. It looked like a run through the left side. But Bettis fooled the Rams. He cut through a hole on the right.

Now Bettis was out in the secondary, the defensive backfield. He shook off one tackler. Then he cut back to the left side and outraced two more defenders.

Fifty yards later, Bettis was in the end zone for a touchdown. The Steelers were on their way to a 42–6 victory.

"That's a big play," Bettis said. "That's not a 5-yard run. That's a long play."

It was his longest run in the NFL since he had dashed 71 yards as a rookie with the Rams. Bettis was back.

# School of Hard Knocks

Jerome Bettis was born on February 16, 1972. He lived in a two-story brick home in Detroit, Michigan. Football was not his first love. At the age of seven, he took up bowling. "I grew up bowling, bowling, bowling," Bettis said. At thirteen, he went into football with the same spark.

Jerome grew up playing street football in Detroit. He still has scars from those rough games.

"It was tackle on the grass, touch on the street, but they'd still hit you on the cement," Bettis says. "The only equipment we had was a football."

His mother did not want Jerome to play football in high school. She thought her son would be hurt. She changed her mind after a talk with her brother, Jerome's uncle. He was a football coach in Detroit.

"He was out in the streets playing football one day," Gladys Bettis said. "My brother was watching Jerome play. He said, 'That boy's got talent.'"

Jerome was soon on the high school team. There was only one way his mother would let him play. He had to keep up with his schoolwork. To Gladys Bettis and her husband, Johnnie, Jr., that was

Jerome always made sure his mother knew he was okay after he was tackled in high school.

more important than anything. They wanted each of their three children, Jerome, Johnnie III, and Kimberly, to go to college.

Jerome's mother did not know much about football. But Jerome and Johnnie taught her the game. When Jerome began playing at Mackenzie High School, she was his biggest fan. But she was still worried he would get hurt. Jerome was once tackled very hard and looked like he was hurt. But he quickly jumped to his feet. He searched the stands for his mom and gave her a sign that he was OK. Every time he was tackled hard, he did the same thing.

Hard-hitting was the only way to describe Bettis's play in high school. He played both tight end and nose guard in the tenth grade. At halftime at one of the games, an angry man came rushing into the Mackenzie locker room. It was the coach for the other team. "You leave Bettis in there [the game]," he told Mackenzie coach Bob Dozier, "and he's going to kill somebody."

Jerome's brother knew what Dozier meant. Once, while the two were playing street football, Jerome had turned the corner between the curb and sidewalk. He came straight at Johnnie, full speed. "I lowered my shoulder to tackle him," Johnnie said. "He about took it off and kept going."

In his last two years in high school, Jerome played running back. He lifted weights. He pushed cars up driveways to build up his leg strength. At 235 pounds, he could run over players just as he had bowled over his brother. In his senior year, he was named the No. 1 high school player in Michigan. College offers poured in.

"I looked at my chances and decided I wanted to play fullback," he said.

Notre Dame promised him he could play that position.

# A Sweet Performance

Football practice opened at Notre Dame for the 1990 season with Jerome Bettis on the injured list.

Bettis had hurt his leg in a high school all-star game. When he finally returned, he did not play much as a freshman at Notre Dame. "It took a long time for me to come back from that [injury]," Bettis said. "For me not to be able to practice, it's like they scratch your name out." But Bettis did show promise by rushing for 115 yards on only fifteen carries. He also scored a touchdown.

In his second year at Notre Dame, Bettis was not sure if he would play much. But coach Lou Holtz remembered a game in the spring of 1990. On one play, a defender tried to stop

**In his second year of college, Jerome Bettis set a Notre Dame record after scoring twenty touchdowns.**

Bettis at the goal line. Bettis sent the player flying into the end zone. Bettis showed the same kind of power in the few times he carried the ball as a freshman. So when Bettis became a sophomore, the Notre Dame coach made him the starting fullback.

Bettis made his first college start against Indiana. He rushed for 111 yards on just ten carries. Then he ran for 93 yards against Michigan State. Against Stanford, he had 179 yards and four touchdowns. Against Southern Cal, Bettis rushed for 178 yards and two touchdowns. Against Pitt, 125 yards and two touchdowns. The high yardage kept coming. By the end of the season, Bettis had scored twenty touchdowns and totaled 120 points—both Notre Dame records.

The Notre Dame Fighting Irish had one of the top teams in the country. They were headed for the Sugar Bowl. They were playing the Florida Gators. The Gators had won eight straight games. It was going to be Florida's great passing attack against Notre Dame's powerful ground game.

By the fourth quarter, the Gators led, 22–17. Time was running out for Notre Dame.

There were less than five minutes left. Notre Dame had the ball on the 3-yard line. Jerome Bettis raced toward the end zone for a touchdown. Notre Dame went for the two-point conversion and went in front, 25–22.

Jerome Bettis turns downfield with his eyes on the end zone.

Bettis scored again with 3:32 left. This time, he raced 49 yards. The Gators kept the game close. They scored a touchdown to make it 32–28. They

were now only four points behind the Fighting Irish.

With two minutes left, Bettis roared 39 yards for another touchdown. He had scored three touchdowns in less than three minutes. Notre Dame beat Florida, 39–28. Bettis was voted the game's most valuable player.

Now Jerome Bettis was ready for his junior year.

# Bowling Them Over

Suddenly, Jerome Bettis was in the spotlight. People stopped him on the street to ask for his autograph or just to shake his hand. People said he might be in the running for the Heisman Trophy. The Heisman Trophy is given each year to the best college football player in America.

Coaches called Bettis the best fullback in the country. Defenders tried to stop him, but it was not easy.

"Any time you can put a 250-pound man at running back and have him run straight ahead, that's impressive," said Pitt coach Paul Hackett. He had just seen Bettis score three touchdowns against his team on runs of 8, 2, and 11 yards. Notre Dame won, 52–21.

When Bettis did not run for 100 yards or score a couple of touchdowns in a game, it was news. It was also news when Notre Dame lost. So everyone wondered about Bettis and Notre Dame after a 33–16 loss to Stanford. The usually sure-handed Bettis had lost two fumbles and only gained 54 yards. Bettis missed the game against Navy because he had

Even though he missed part of the season, Jerome Bettis rushed for over 700 yards in his junior year of college.

hurt his ankle. And he lost his starting spot for three other games. Tailback Reggie Brooks took over the spotlight at Notre Dame.

Once Bettis came back from his injury, he was hard to stop. By the end of his junior season, he had rushed for over 700 yards. He had reached one of his goals even though he had missed part of the season.

Bettis also hoped to play in another Bowl game, not to mention win a national championship. If a Heisman Trophy came his way, so much the better.

But missing those games because of injury cost Bettis a chance to win the Heisman. Notre Dame was no longer in the national title race after losing to Stanford. There was still time to make the season great.

Next stop for Notre Dame was the Cotton Bowl and mighty Texas A&M. No one had beaten the Aggies all year. For one of the few times during the season, Notre Dame was the underdog. Bettis felt he had to lead the team.

Jerome Bettis skipped his senior year of college to join the NFL.

But in the first half of the game, Bettis played the role of blocking back instead of star runner.

Then came the second half. Bettis swung out of the backfield and raced downfield to catch a pass from Rick Mirer for a touchdown.

Late in the third quarter, Bettis smashed over from the 1-yard line. Then he scored again on a 4-yard sprint. Bettis led Notre Dame to a 28–3 upset.

Next stop for Bettis was the NFL. He skipped his senior year at Notre Dame to join the pros.

# A Battering Ram

There's no stopping me. No, no no," Jerome Bettis yelled at the New Orleans Saints.

The Rams were hoping for big things from Bettis after picking him in the 1993 NFL draft. He did not let them down.

Against the Saints, the Rams' rookie ran 71 yards for a touchdown. He outraced four quick defenders for the score. He went for more yardage. He was all around the field.

"(The yards) were coming so quick, I couldn't add that quickly," Bettis said.

By the end of the day, Bettis had rushed for 212 yards. It was only the eighth time in NFL history that a rookie had gone over the 200-yard mark in a game. Bettis might have had more except he had an asthma attack. He sat on the sidelines in the second quarter.

Bettis was all too familiar with asthma. He had played football with the condition ever since high school. One day as a freshman at football practice, he found it hard to fill his lungs with air. The more he tried to breathe, the worse it got. His chest was tight and got tighter. Then his world went dark. "I passed out," he remembered.

It did not keep Bettis from continuing to play football. "My parents said, 'Don't let this change your plans. If you want to play football, you can.'"

Asthma did not stop him in the NFL, either. In one game in 1997, Bettis had been slammed to the ground. When he tried to get to his feet, he knew something was wrong. "I couldn't breathe," he said. "I

Jerome Bettis does not let his asthma stop him from playing.

was scared." Bettis was carried off the field on a stretcher. But Jerome Bettis was back in action slamming into the line again. He had no fear.

"It bothers me sometimes," Bettis said of his asthma. "I have an inhaler on the sidelines in case I need it and the doctors and trainers are there."

Big rushing totals were not new for Bettis in his first season in the NFL. No one expected him to battle for the league rushing title. Fullbacks are powerful runners, but they rarely win rushing titles. They are usually used when a couple of tough yards are needed. Rushing titles usually go to the speedier tailbacks. But guess what? With two weeks left in the season, Bettis was leading the league in rushing.

"I wasn't just the bruising, battering fullback-type of runner that everybody thought I was," Bettis said.

It was the last day of the season. The Rams did all they could to help Bettis win the rushing title. They handed him the ball a team record of thirty-nine times. He rushed for 146 yards against the Chicago Bears. But he fell 58 yards short of the rushing title.

Still, Bettis's total of 1,429 yards was impressive. It was no surprise that he was named the NFL's Rookie of the Year. Bettis played in the Pro Bowl game against the league's best players.

In his second season, Bettis handed out t-shirts to his teammates that said, "2,000 or

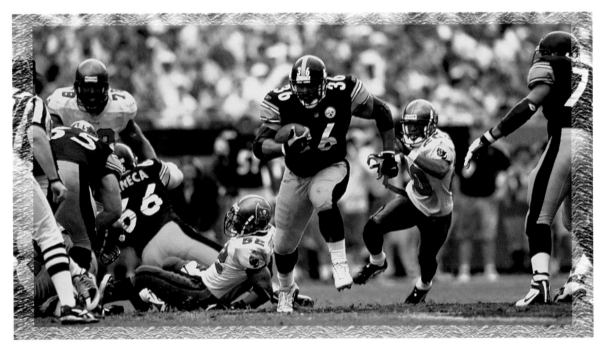

The Rams traded Bettis to the Pittsburgh Steelers in 1996.

Bust." His goal was to rush for 2,000 yards. He came up short. But he still rushed for over 1,000 even though defenders were piling up on him. His 1,025 yards earned him another spot in the Pro Bowl. He was the only member of his team to make the NFL's all-star game in Hawaii. Although the NFC lost the game, Bettis led the NFC in rushing yardage.

Jerome Bettis was doing great. But, in 1995, a contract battle and injuries added up to a below-average season for Bettis. Bettis found himself playing for a new team in 1996. The Rams traded Bettis to the Pittsburgh Steelers.

CHAPTER 6

# Bettis Is Back

Jerome Bettis was excited. It was the first time he had played in the NFL's Monday Night Game.

"With the Rams, we didn't get too many games on national TV," he said. "People didn't know much about me."

Football fans quickly found out about the Pittsburgh Steelers' new running back. The Steelers were playing the Buffalo Bills.

The Steelers handed the ball to Bettis. He was off. He ran five yards, and then ten. He was out in the secondary. Four Buffalo defenders had a chance to knock him down. He scored after racing 43 yards. It was the Steelers' longest scoring run since 1992.

Bettis finished the night with 133 rushing yards and two touchdowns. The Steelers beat the Bills, 24–6.

It was Bettis's second straight 100-yard game for the Steelers. After only three games, Bettis was already nearly halfway to his entire yardage total for the 1995 season with the Rams.

"I'm in running back heaven right now," Bettis said.

He was even happier after beating the Rams. He had shown his former team he was not finished. On one run against the Rams, Bettis knocked over several players. He glared over at the St. Louis sideline.

"I wanted them to get a good look at me," he said.

After only eight games, Bettis was well on his way to another 1,000-yard season. He finished the 1996 season with 1,431 rushing yards. He was second in the league and was named the Steelers' Most Valuable Player by his teammates.

The Steelers fans loved Bettis. He became one of the most popular athletes in Pittsburgh. Just like at Notre Dame, he was nicknamed "The Bus" for his hard running style. The Steelers fans cheered whenever they saw a picture of a bus on the scoreboard. That meant Bettis had just made a big play.

The season ended for the Steelers with a playoff loss. This was a team that had played in the Super Bowl the year before. But the Steelers had gained quite a prize in Bettis.

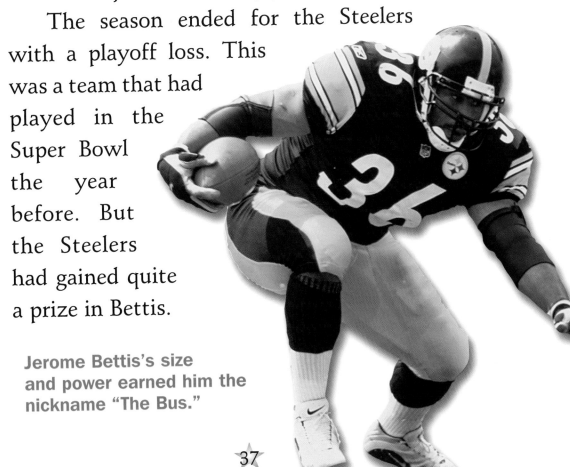

Jerome Bettis's size and power earned him the nickname "The Bus."

# Home to Stay

"Take the Bus." The words were on a banner hanging in one end zone at Three Rivers Stadium. Pittsburgh Steelers fans were saying: Give the ball to Jerome Bettis.

The Steelers did and Bettis did the rest. In a game against the Washington Redskins, he rushed for 134 yards. The Steelers won, 14–13.

It was the 1997

season and there was more to come. By the end of the season, Bettis had rushed for a career-high 1,665 yards. He carried the Steelers to a division title.

"The Bus" showed no signs of slowing down. He won team MVP awards in 1996, 1997, and 2000. He had 1,185 yards in 1998; 1,091 yards in 1999; and 1,341 in 2000.

After the 2000 season, Bettis was a free agent. He could sign with any team. Steelers fans were thrilled when he decided to stay in Pittsburgh. He signed a new contract for $30 million over six years. He hoped to stay in Pittsburgh for the rest of his career. "My new contract will enable me to retire as a Steeler," Bettis said.

As well as playing football, Jerome Bettis also spends time working with his charity to help needy children.

## ★ UP CLOSE

In 2001, Jerome Bettis became the fourteenth runner to have more than 10,000 rushing yards.

By the end of the 2001 season, Bettis had brought his career total to 10,876.

Bettis had become a Pittsburgh star, but it was not only for his football talents. He is known for a wide variety of charity work. In 1997, he started "The Bus Stops Here Foundation" to help needy children. He has worked to save neighborhood parks and recreation centers. He has hosted summer youth football camps. His work on and off the field was recognized by the NFL. In 2000, Jerome Bettis earned the Walter Payton NFL Man of the Year award. He also had a weekly television show. There are food products with his nickname all over town. He is as much a part of Pittsburgh as the steelworkers. Pittsburgh is famous for making steel, that is why it is called the "Steel City."

Bettis feels right at home in Pittsburgh. "It's

Jerome Bettis is right at home in Pittsburgh and will remain there for the rest of his career in the NFL.

a blue-collar town and I'm a blue-collar player," he said. "I'm not a flashy guy."

The fans like him because he never gives up. They like his courage and style. No matter how much he hurts after getting tackled, he will get up and give it another try. He is like a bus, as he says, a "big, bad bruising kind of thing that carries people."

Bettis has become someone to look up to in the NFL for players and fans.

# CAREER STATISTICS

| Rushing | | | | | | |
|---|---|---|---|---|---|---|
| Year | Team | GP | Att. | Yds. | Avg. | TDs |
| 1993 | St. Louis | 16 | 294 | 1,429 | 4.9 | 7 |
| 1994 | St. Louis | 16 | 319 | 1,025 | 3.2 | 3 |
| 1995 | St. Louis | 15 | 183 | 637 | 3.5 | 3 |
| 1996 | Pittsburgh | 16 | 320 | 1,431 | 4.5 | 11 |
| 1997 | Pittsburgh | 15 | 375 | 1,665 | 4.4 | 7 |
| 1998 | Pittsburgh | 15 | 316 | 1,185 | 3.8 | 3 |
| 1999 | Pittsburgh | 16 | 299 | 1,091 | 3.6 | 7 |
| 2000 | Pittsburgh | 16 | 355 | 1,341 | 3.8 | 8 |
| 2001 | Pittsburgh | 11 | 225 | 1,072 | 4.8 | 4 |
| **Totals** | | **136** | **2,686** | **10,876** | **4.0** | **53** |

| Recieving | | | | | | |
|---|---|---|---|---|---|---|
| Year | Team | GP | Rec. | Yds. | Avg. | TDs |
| 1993 | St. Louis | 16 | 26 | 244 | 9.4 | 0 |
| 1994 | St. Louis | 16 | 31 | 293 | 9.5 | 1 |
| 1995 | St. Louis | 15 | 18 | 106 | 5.9 | 0 |
| 1996 | Pittsburgh | 16 | 22 | 122 | 5.5 | 0 |
| 1997 | Pittsburgh | 15 | 15 | 110 | 7.3 | 2 |
| 1998 | Pittsburgh | 15 | 16 | 90 | 5.6 | 0 |
| 1999 | Pittsburgh | 16 | 21 | 110 | 5.2 | 0 |
| 2000 | Pittsburgh | 16 | 13 | 97 | 7.5 | 0 |
| 2001 | Pittsburgh | 11 | 8 | 48 | 6.0 | 0 |
| **Totals** | | **136** | **170** | **1,220** | **7.2** | **3** |

**GP**—Games Played
**Rec.**—Receptions
**Att.**—Rushing attempts

**Yds.**—Receiving/Rushing
**Avg.**—Average
**TDs**—Touchdowns

# Where to Write to Jerome Bettis

Mr. Jerome Bettis
c/o The Pittsburgh Steelers
3400 South Water Street
Pittsburgh, PA 15203-2349

Bettis has become someone to look up to in the NFL for both players and fans.

# WORDS TO KNOW

**draft**—A selection of players by teams, who take turns choosing the players they want.

**freshman**—A ninth-grade student in high school or a first-year student in college.

**fullback**—The fullback is normally called upon whenever short yardage is needed. He is usually the most powerful runner on the team. He can drive straight ahead into the line or block for other runners.

**Heisman Trophy**—The award that is given each year to the best college football player in America.

**junior**—An eleventh-grade student in high school or a third-year student in college.

**nose guard**—A defensive player who usually lines up over center.

**quarterback**—He is in charge of the offense. He calls the plays, sometimes with help from the bench. The quarterback can either pass the ball, hand it off to a running back, or keep it and run.

**rookie**—A player in his first full season in professional sports.

secondary—If a runner gets past the line of scrimmage, he has to get past the players in the secondary further downfield.

senior—A twelfth-grade student in high school or a fourth-year student in college.

sophomore—A tenth-grade student in high school or a second-year student in college.

Super Bowl—The NFL's championship game.

tailback—A quick runner who is usually lighter and faster than the fullback. He most often slashes through openings in the line or runs outside, and for longer yardage.

tight end—Usually a big player who catches passes and blocks for runners.

# READING ABOUT

## Books

Italia, Bob. *The Pittsburgh Steelers.* Minneapolis, Minn.: ABDO Publishing Company, 1996.

Lace, William H. *The Pittsburgh Steelers Football Team.* Berkeley Heights, N.J.: Enslow Publishers, Inc., 1999.

Nelson, Julie and Michael E. Goodman. *Pittsburgh Steelers.* Mankato, Minn.: Creative Education, 2000.

O'Brien, Jim. *Keep the Faith: The Steelers of Two Different Eras.* Pittsburgh, Penn.: James P. O'Brien Publishing, 1997.

## Internet Addresses

*The Official Web Site of Jerome Bettis*
    <http://www.thebus36.com>

*The Official Web Site of the Pittsburgh Steelers: Jerome Bettis*
    <http://www.steelers.com/team/
    playerpage.cfm?player_id=4834>

# INDEX